First Facts™

Learning about Money

Spending Money

by Mary Firestone

Consultant:
Sharon M. Danes, PhD
Professor and Family Economist
University of Minnesota

Capstone
press
Mankato, Minnesota

First Facts is published by Capstone Press
151 Good Counsel Drive, P.O. Box 669, Mankato, Minnesota 56002
www.capstonepress.com

Library of Congress Cataloging-in-Publication Data
Firestone, Mary.
    Spending money / by Mary Firestone.
    p. cm. (First facts. Learning about money.)
    Includes bibliographical references and index.
    ISBN 0-7368-2641-6 (hardcover)
    1. Finance, Personal—Juvenile literature. 2. Money—Juvenile literature. 3. Children—Finance,
Personal—Juvenile literature. I. Title.
HG179.F5332 2005
332.024′0083—dc22   2004000408

Summary: Explores the principles and choice involved with spending money as well
    as showing different ways of paying with money, such as checks and credit cards.

Editorial Credits
Heather Adamson, editor; Jennifer Bergstrom, designer; Enoch Peterson, illustrator;
    Scott Thoms, photo researcher; Eric Kudalis, product planning editor

Photo Credits
Capstone Press/Gary Sundermeyer, 5 (foreground), 8, 9, 11, 16, 17, 19 (foreground)
Comstock Inc., 1 (all)
Corbis/AFP, 20; Chuck Savage, 6–7; Layne Kennedy, 10;
Image Ideas, 5 (background)
Ingram Publishing, front cover
PhotoDisc Inc., back cover, 12–13 (crayons), 19 (background)
SuperStock/Francisco Cruz, 14

1 2 3 4 5 6 09 08 07 06 05 04

Table of Contents

Spending Money

Today, Pat paid 75 cents for ice cream from the store. Last week, he paid $1 for ice cream from an ice-cream truck. Pat saved 25 cents by changing where he buys ice cream. Spending carefully helps people save money.

Fun Fact!
Americans spend more than $9 billion on ice cream each year.

People Need Money

People **need** money. They use it to buy things they need to live, such as food. People also use money for things they **want**, such as music CDs. People may also use their money to help others. Careful spending lets people buy the things they need and want.

Fun Fact!
An average U.S. family of three spends $507 a month on groceries.

Costs

Sometimes items that are alike have different **prices**. Some items cost more because they are made better. They will last longer, so they are worth more.

Some items cost more only because they are **popular**. Famous people may help sell these items. Pat compares all **brands** before he spends his money.

Choices

Most people do not earn enough
money to buy everything they want.
People must decide how to spend their
money. They make **choices**.

Pat and his family choose to share their money. Some people do not have enough money for food or clothes. Pat's family helps them by sharing.

Money Plans

Money plans help people spend money carefully. Pat keeps track of how much he spends. He decides how much to save and how much he wants to share. When Pat earns money, he follows his money plan.

Fun Fact!
Nearly half of U.S. children who are 8 to 14 years old receive allowances.

What I will earn:

allowance
yard work
dog walking $10
total = $10
             $5
           $25

How I will spend:

savings
pet food
share with others $5
new bike fund $4
ice cream $5
            $8
total = $3
          $25

Checks

Checks let people use the money they keep at banks. Checks are pieces of paper shaped like dollars.

Pat's mom uses checks to pay bills. She writes in the business name and amount of the bill. Then, she signs the check. The bank uses her money to pay the store.

Fun Fact!
Checks come in many colors and styles. Some have cartoon characters or sports team logos.

Credit

Credit is borrowed money. Using credit, people can buy things now and pay for them later. Pat's dad uses a credit card to buy new work boots.

People pay extra if they do not pay back credit on time. Pat's dad gets paid each week. He uses his paycheck money to pay the credit card company.

Be a Good Spender

People must spend money carefully.
Then they will have enough money for
their needs and wants. Pat checks
prices. He uses a money plan. He saves
enough money to buy ice cream for
a friend.

Amazing but True!

Todd McFarlane paid $3 million for a baseball. The ball was hit by Mark McGwire of the St. Louis Cardinals. It was from McGwire's 70th home run during the 1998 season.

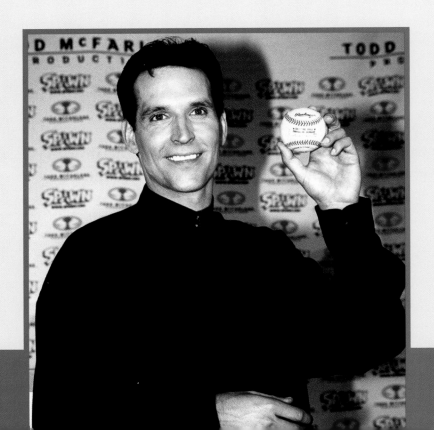

Hands On: Shop Smart

Comparing prices can help you spend less money. Have an adult help you find the best price by reading ads and visiting a store.

What You Need

newspaper ads from a local store
pencil
paper

What You Do

1. Find an interesting item in a store's newspaper ad. Write down what you know about the item. Write down questions for things you don't know.
2. Go to the store and look carefully at the item. See if you can find answers to your questions. If you need help, ask a store worker.
3. Look in the store for other items like the one in the ad. Write down the different prices. Write down any other differences in the items such as size or quality.
4. Look at your list of prices and items. Which item has the lowest price? Which item has the best quality? Decide which item gives you the most for the money.

Glossary

brand (BRAND)—a company name or a name of a product

choice (CHOISS)—picking or selecting from several things

credit (KRED-it)—money borrowed to buy something; people must pay credit back later.

need (NEED)—to require something; you need food, shelter, and clothes to stay alive.

popular (POP-yuh-lur)—liked or wanted by many people

price (PRISSE)—the amount you have to pay for something

want (WONT)—to feel you would like to have something; you may want a new bike or a snack.

Read More

Rosinsky, Natalie M. *Spending Money*. Let's See Library. Minneapolis: Compass Point Books, 2004.

Thayer, Tanya. *Spending Money*. First Step Nonfiction. Minneapolis: Lerner, 2002.

Internet Sites

FactHound offers a safe, fun way to find Internet sites related to this book. All of the sites on FactHound have been researched by our staff.

Here's how:
1. Visit *www.facthound.com*
2. Type in this special code **0736826416** for age-appropriate sites. Or enter a search word related to this book for a more general search.
3. Click on the **Fetch It** button.

FactHound will fetch the best sites for you!

Index